Manifestation Through
The Power Of Mysticism
2023 ©
Author Michele Blood
VIDEO BOOK and E-Book
VIDEOS Created By Holly Fallah

Published by Michele's MusiVation Int'l
PO Box 12933
La Jolla, California 92037
USA
All rights reserved.
Printed in the United States of America
ISBN: 978-1-890679-82-8

This book may not be copied, duplicated or used in any way without the written permission of the publishers.

For wholesale copies
email team@TheMysticalExperience.com

Cover art by H.Fallah and M.Blood

*This Manifestation Video Book
is dedicated to you.*

*The Divine knows who you are and
what your heart longs to experience.*

*So, we dedicate this Video Book
to your enlightenment, your
prosperity, health, and happiness.*

*You are not alone,
and you are so loved.*

Table Of Contents

Introduction 1
Manifesting Through The Power Of Love 5
Meditation and Prosperity 9
Are You A Mystic? 22
The Power of Intuition 36
The Power of Meditation 39
How To Become Enlightened 46
What Is Consciousness?.............................. 53
The Pole of Prosperity................................ 58
Six Steps To Achieving Your Big Vision 63
Affirmation Power 74
Divine Guidance or Emotion from Ego? 86
Psychic Phenomena versus True Intuition 92
Six Methods To Uplift Your Vibration.......... 100
Link To All The Affirmation Songs.............. 109

Introduction

"We are what we think. All that we are arises with our thoughts. With our thoughts, we make the world." The Buddha said this two and half thousand years ago. So, it's no secret that what we think about creates our reality. It's with our thoughts we create the world. You can use your thoughts through positive affirmations, visualizations, meditation, and music. With a combination of all four methods, it only takes a few weeks to a few months to turn your entire life to the positive.

Hello, this is Michele Blood and I have been teaching manifestation, visualization, meditation, and affirmation music for over 30 years. I have worked with the late, great Bob Proctor. We co-created many positive seminars, products and books together over many years. I've shared the stage internationally with Dr. Deepak Chopra, Dr. Wayne Dyer, Louise Haye, and many other great people. I've been doing this for a long time. I started as a musician, as a rock singer in Australia, and after a near fatal car accident I had a life-changing epiphany. A life-changing epiphany that not only healed my body when I was in the hospital, but created great, worldwide success and has helped millions of people worldwide to wake up to the true nature of their life, their true purpose, and how they can manifest as well.

I know that you want a better, richer, happier, healthier, and more successful life. I know this, for deep inside we all do. And that's why I congratulate you. You're not one of the millions who are sitting at home, night after night in front of the TV. Hoping and praying that one day, maybe if they win the lottery. If only they do this, if only they do that. "Everybody else is just lucky," they say. But do you know what luck stands for? Luck stands for Learning and Loving Under Correct Knowledge.

So, when you are prepared in consciousness to accept prosperity and to be healed, then true, positive change will be your experience. You are a magnet through your thoughts. However, my friends, what I do know, and I know this for a fact. When you add visuals, when you're listening to an audio program and you can see beautiful pictures right in front of you, because the mind thinks in pictures, well then, the manifestation works 300 times faster than any other method to change your life. And all my great and positive, worldwide, successful affirmation songs are at the end of this Video Book after every chapter. So, you are getting so much with this Video Book. Isn't it marvelous, a Video Book. You get to hear what I'm saying but you get to also see all of the transcription, you get the eBook, and "Manifestation Through The Power Of Mysticism," this Video Book, is so powerful.

Every single chapter has a special, visual video to go with what I'm speaking about, and you also get the eBook. And you can also, if you'd like, get the printed book if you want that as well. This entire program is going to turn your life around 360 degrees. Because if you really want positive change, and you want positive change fast, you've got to use all of these manifestation tools. Visualization is what we're giving to you. All you have to do is listen and watch the Video Book. That's all you have to do, and it will enter the treasury of your subconscious mind, and eventually manifest into your experience. And if you want to follow along, you can follow along with the eBook. You just take all of this in. Watch all these chapters, watch this Video Book over and over and over. And I cover so much amazing, life-changing information from Intuition, Manifestation, to Meditation, to everything that you ever wanted to know about consciousness and how to change your life.

You are about to become the most positive person you've ever met. You are going to begin to see opportunities and success, and you will know how to take action. You will begin to be a magnet to money and so much more. This is the best product that we have ever created along with our Magnet To Money App team. The Magnet To Money App is what has inspired us to do this for you. Our team has put together everything that will raise your consciousness through the Magnet To Money App and through this Manifestation Through The Power Of Mysticism Video Book. As your mind takes in the visual pictures, you will begin to see yourself with higher consciousness, with more prosperity, and you will be growing in leaps and bounds. To learn about all these amazing topics, these topics will allow you to open your heart and your mind to the impossible becoming possible in your life.

So, I welcome you today to the "Manifestation Through The Power Of Mysticism" Video Book. Your life is about to change for the positive, and I am so happy for you, and I AM with you.

In Love and Oneness,
Michele

As a reminder, if you have this eBook, print book, or audiobook without already having the Powerful Video Book, you can go to the following link to get the Manifestation Through The Power Of Mysticism Video Book at a discount. Just go to: www.MagnetToSuccess.com/ManifestationVideoBook

Then add the Video Book to your cart. On the checkout page click the link that says "Have a coupon? Click here to enter your code" and enter the following coupon code on the checkout page.

More Love *(Is the code)*

Manifesting Through The Power Of Love

Dear One! Why do I address you as "Dear One"? Because we are all one, therefore very close and dear to each other. In this first chapter I would like to share some ideas, heartfelt love, and information about manifesting through the power of letting go and, of course, the Power of Love.

I know it's important to be quiet and let go. Not just for our peace of mind, however, also to let the power flow through us so that we get out of the way. Sometimes, our good simply wants to catch up with us, and it can do so when we take the time to be quiet, relax, and let go.

We can simply turn our attention away from all the things we want to manifest in the 3rd dimension, or outer world, and go within to bring them forth. Let us all do as the great Thomas Troward did and ask for more of God in us than us! Be open to receiving and experiencing more peace, more awareness, more love, and compassion. May there be more of God in me than me.

When we do this, we will find that the walls we have built, which appear to obstruct us from realizing our dreams, begin to crumble, and our truth and dreams start to become a reality. The walls will disappear because it was an illusion. When we do this, what we do want to manifest will not evaporate; it will last, grow, and build. This way, we will ALWAYS, in ALL RIGHT WAYS, feel fulfilled, on purpose, and be prosperous and happy.

The love we seek, the prosperity we seek, the passion for life we seek, not only is seeking us; it is us. As the Mystical and beautiful Poet Rumi said, "Out beyond the ideas of wrongdoing and right doing there is a field, I'll meet you there." When we let go and be still, a molecular structure grows which will meet us on this field of the 3rd dimension.

How do we meet our good to manifest in the field?

1) FIRST, sit down somewhere quiet, preferably outside in nature or even out on a balcony as I often do, as long as you can feel you can sit there in peace and quiet.

So now take ten deep breaths in through the nose and out through the mouth. Do this by breathing in through the nose and out through the mouth slowly, and as you are doing this think these words: "Peace. I AM Peace!"

2) Then close your eyes and say out loud, *"I am peace. I am joy. I am love. I am compassion. I*

am health. I am wealth. I am beautiful. I am aware. I am that I am!" There does not have to be an order to it, simply say positive words out loud and then breathe, relax, and let go.

3) Next say in your own words...
"Dear Infinite one, today I turn away from my old self and begin anew. I now go within to where I know all that is required to live a truly happy, prosperous life is now made manifest. I now call into my life all the good there is and release everyone and everything that is not for my highest good, to their highest good."

4) Then begin to visualize what it is you DO want as if it has already happened. Watching this Video Book with the beautiful images will greatly assist with this.

Get into that feeling that you NOW have all that you require to have a beautiful life.

5) Keep breathing, relax, quiet the mind, and let go. And let God. If you are still having a challenge with quieting the mind chatter, keep repeating to yourself in your mind.
"I am that I am. I am peace. I am joy. I am love. I am compassion. I am health. I am wealth. I am beautiful. I am aware. I am that I am! Thank you for my beautiful life!"

Whenever we feel we have to look outside of ourselves for love, please know that all of the love we could ever handle in a million, billion lifetimes is there pouring itself into, through, and all around us when we let go.

May Love bless you today, tonight, and always, and may your spiritual awareness always guide you and rise with every passing moment.
Remember The Divine Presence Has Gone Before You To Prepare The Way.

Through Meditation You Can Become Prosperous

I would love for you to really tune in to this Chapter, because it may be the key to your new understanding of money and spirituality, and what is happening behind the scenes with the beautiful, Eternal, Holy Light. This Light is the oscillating vibration of the Divine. The title says it all, through meditation you can indeed become prosperous.

Now, let's get into what this means for your life. Some people tend to become very perplexed about prosperity and spirituality and think it doesn't mix. However, the practice of meditation will not only assist you to become prosperous, gain energy, and become healthier; it will also be your ticket to freedom. Freed-OM.

I have been teaching metaphysics and deep mysticism since the early '90s. I was a pop singer in Australia, touring all around Australia. One day I had a near-fatal car accident which actually changed my life for the better. Not everything that appears to be negative is *truly* negative. The car accident took me in a new direction towards my true purpose. However, you don't have to go through something horrific to have good things happen in your life. It's our attitude towards what happens in life which helps us learn and better ourselves at every moment.

It wasn't until I started writing positive affirmation songs that I was on my way to becoming healed from my car accident. I started writing more positive affirmation songs that I called "Affirmation Power" music. Later it was retitled Musivation™. Bob Proctor's wife, Linda, came up with the name Musivation™, which is motivation and music combined. Affirmations absolutely change your thoughts, and this changes your life. With the music, the affirmations are planted into your subconscious 300 times faster than simply saying or writing them down.

That was how my journey to my soul's purpose began. I was creating metaphysical, positive, affirmation music and singing it all over Australia and the world. I worked and shared the stage with wonderful Teachers from all over the world including Bob Proctor, Deepak Chopra, Wayne Dyer, Stuart Wilde and so many other inspiring authors. I was living an amazing life; however, I was still searching for something more. So, I started meditation practice, climbing incredible mountains, and going through dangerous jungles to find God in my life; to find that Divine. I had this heart glow that wouldn't stop. I was living with this overpowering urge to find the Divine. I was in love. So, I went searching for the Divine and eventually, I found my path to Truth. I won't go into all the details in this chapter. You can always go to www.TheMysticalExperience.com if you want to read more about my journey.

I was so blessed to eventually, after many years and many countries, meet someone who knew God, an Enlightened Teacher. Her name is Kundalini. I was so blessed that she agreed to teach me and eventually I awakened. My own Kundalini awakened because when you have a True Teacher, they can Transmit Light to you. And, if you meditate as well, the combination assists you to go into higher states of being that you may never have been able to reach on your own. You know that old saying, "You have to do it on your own, however, you cannot do it alone." Now I teach meditation and mysticism to people from all over the world, from all walks of life, and of all ages.

It doesn't matter who you are or what you do, your entire circumstances can be uplifted through Meditation practice. Whether you're an atheist, agnostic or you truly are a seeker of truth on the path, the practice of meditation can assist you and bring up your oscillation, your Divine vibration.

So, that's why we're going to speak now about meditation and how it can make you prosperous in every area of your life.

My intention for you is that now today, in every moment that you're reading this and when you watch the Video Book, your vibration, your oscillation, becomes faster, a higher Divine frequency. This gives you energy, clarity of mind, and creativity, which is how people become successful. They have their spiritual momentum turned UP.

Meditation and spirituality are the same. Meditation and money are the same. Spirituality and prosperity are the same. Why do people have it in their heads that if you are spiritual you should live in poverty? That may be true in the East where people understand and feed and look after souls on their journey to awakening. However, in the West, we must look after ourselves. So, in fact, the more you are one with the Divine, the more you can co-create a beautiful life. Allow the Divine who is your true consciousness, to co-create beauty and love into this beautiful world. Your purpose here on this planet is to co-create with the Divine and become FREE. If the Divine is living through your body and your body is the temple of the Divine, then your life and your body must be looked after.

If you are living in poverty or you don't have enough for your family and your loved ones, what happens is that your oscillation goes down. Your energy goes down, and then it gets harder and harder to do the things that need to be done. Some find as their energy goes down it also affects their health and attitude. They find it easier to complain and be negative because then at least, at an unconscious level, that negativity can temporally relieve their suffering. They start complaining about other people and never have a nice word to say. And you know when people are doing this they are living in fear. We must have compassion because they are not happy people. However, they CAN BE HAPPY again.

That is another reason why I love to teach people that prosperity is not a dirty word. Wealth is good, and I am speaking about wealth in every area of your life. This includes wealth in health, or wealth in seeing the beauty all around you. Every leaf on every tree is prosperity. This also includes wealth in your bank accounts. Why would you buy a little cheap mattress, or cheap little pillows, when you spend so much time in bed? Someone was raving on, "Oh, I've got this bed for only 200 bucks and pillows for five bucks." This is not a way to live. This isn't something to brag about.

You've got to live a life that is good, that is honoring the Divine through you. You're not doing it for egotistical reasons. And we must honor people who are really making it in this world successfully, because you will see by their demeanor, by their energy, by their oscillation, by their generosity, where their consciousness is; you can feel their love for life.

When I was writing my own affirmation songs for my healing, I heard this tape from this man called Reverend Ike, a preacher in New York. However, I had never heard of such a preacher before. WOW, he blew my socks off with his positivity about prosperity. And I listened to this tape repeatedly, and he kept saying, "Spirituality and money are wonderful. You are a magnet to money. Everyone say right now, 'Money loves me and loves to be around me and circulate. Money loves me.'" So, I went home that night, and I wrote this affirmation song called "I Am A Magnet To Money: Money, Money Loves Me."

As I kept listening to it, it was shifting my paradigm about money. Because I was on my search for God, I wasn't thinking about money. But I noticed my meditation practice was more peaceful. My mind was becoming more still, and things were shifting in my life to the positive. Subtly at first, however, I noticed I was making more and more money. I was working with all of these amazing, world-renowned spiritual and motivational speakers like Bob Proctor, Wayne Dyer, Stuart Wilde, and so many others. No one had done affirmation music in this way, so people hired me to sing at their large events and speak about what I then called "Affirmation Power".

Eventually, I met Reverend Ike and had his permission to release my Magnet To Money song, so wherever I put this song I would always put 'Dedicated To Rev. Ike.' I recorded an interview with Rev. Ike which you can listen to for free on www.Youtube.com on the Rev. Ike channel.

Millions of people have loved and listened to the Magnet To Money affirmation song because it's so different and it does shift consciousness. All these affirmation songs I was writing and recording were shifting my consciousness, however, once I started really practicing meditation things started shifting so much more. Ideas would come to me, and I noticed I had more energy. What's energy? It's vibration. My vibration was becoming powerful, and I was feeling the heart glow tingles through my head. I was happy, but I was still on a search for God, however I kept getting these amazingly creative ideas for writing books, and for writing new music.

Before I knew it, I'm running Bob Proctor's business in Asia, helping him get his book, "You Were Born Rich," as a number-one bestseller, and having hits in Asia with my music. We had huge concerts. I know all of this happened because of Meditation and Affirmations and through positive thinking and positive music. I was so into doing all these things and those things brought my oscillation up fast. Fast enough for me to eventually have my dream come true, to meet an Enlightened Teacher, who taught me for over 10 years.

Meditation is good for everyone. Meditation quietens your mind. You are then in tune with your higher self. When you are in tune with your higher self, things start vibrating towards you, and you are oscillating at a higher vibration. So many people don't get the things that they want, even though they think they are using the Law of Attraction, and this is because they're not resonating with it. They don't feel it really in their heart. They don't feel worthy of it, whether it's a girlfriend, a husband, a better job, better money, or multiple streams of income. They can't even conceive of what they could do to have multiple streams of income.

Well, it's easy. Every single person including you, my darling friend, has what it takes. You have the power within yourself. I love the way Thomas Troward said it in "The Hidden Power". I highly recommend that book. Thomas Troward talked about this hidden power you have within yourself. And when he was in India, he practiced meditation, and I'm sure that man became Enlightened. He lived over 100 years ago and was one of the first teachers of new thought. But of course, the daddy of new thought was the Buddha. It wasn't a new thought back then. That was way before Jesus was even born.

Buddha said, "We are what we think. All that we are arises with our thoughts. With our thoughts, we make the world." And you do, however you must be resonating with it. It can't be just a thought. If you have a thought and you don't get the thing you want, you start going down, and you have all these fears. Nevertheless, when you begin to practice meditation and quiet your mind, then when you have those positive thoughts, it has more energy. Mother Meera, an amazing, Enlightened, beautiful soul says this perfectly: "The Divine wants you to have everything in your life that will bring you happiness". And, of course, that includes money. So, begin to really think of yourself as a prosperous, wealthy person; wealthy in friends, wealthy in love, wealthy in compassion, wealthy in tithing, in generosity and giving. The practice of meditation will get you away from your personality, ego-self, and into your Divine Self.

Here is my prayer for you right now...

The Divine presence is omniscient, omnipotent, omnipresent. And I give thanks to the person who is reading this right now. The omniscient Divine knows exactly who you are because the Divine lives in you, as you. So, I give thanks to your Divine presence. I say, "Go before this person and prepare the way. Bring into their experience everything that will bring them happiness, purpose, spiritual fulfillment, harmony, and prosperity. Their life force is you, Divine. And I know that these words that I speak are the truth and are packed and soaked with Divine Light. May every cell of this person's being, every particle, every atom of their consciousness, and in between the atoms, be filled with Divine, Holy Light/Shakti right here, right now. And I know that my words are the truth for this person. May their mind be absolutely peaceful. May their life be joyful. May every moment of their journey from this moment on become higher and higher in oscillation, in joy, in compassion, in generosity of spirit, and in health. Bring them every opportunity that can bring them to their Divine purpose. May they now be able to see it. May the veils of illusion be lifted so that they can feel this joy, this love, and know that the Divine lives in them, through them, and all around them. Thank you, God."

You are so loved. You had just a taste, a touch, which will bring your oscillation up. You will never again after today go back to the vibration you were at before. It may be a very subtle, subtle movement of life-changing for the better, but it will change. I know this truth for you. And I know that the Divine adores you, is you, which is that eternal ocean of Light. As Peter Pan said, "With just a little bit of fairy dust and a happy thought you can fly." You can fly. Everything is possible for you, everything. And you are so loved.

This assists your spiritual momentum, right here, right now. So, imagine doing this all of the time, and practicing meditation every day. If you truly wish to have your oscillation, go up and to be part of the Divine experience, then practice meditation. It will assist you, your loved ones, your friends, and people you work with, and will give you opportunities you never saw before. It will be like you've broken out of your shackles, like getting a "get out of jail free" card. Every day will be freer.

It won't always be easy, but it will be a life worth living. If you wish for that, I highly recommend you go to www.TheMysticalExperience.com and watch the free videos there. Be part of something that will assist you. Have Light transmitted to you whether you believe in God or not. Why not allow your soul to assist you? You are not reading this by accident. There are no accidents in life. I thank my Teacher Kundalini, I thank the lineage, I thank anyone who's ever meditated, and every Buddha.

I have created a visualization for you. This is a visualization, and you are being meditated as you listen to it. It is called, "The Pool Of Enlightened Samadhi", and it is available on The Magnet To Money App.

As your consciousness, which is your soul, which is the Divine mind, vibrates at a higher oscillation, the Divine presence is clearer in your consciousness, and you start attracting good into your life. You start resonating with things that are in a higher oscillation, good experiences, and more money. Visualization is something that you see in your mind's eye. Which is why this Video Book is so powerful. It's like taking a positive thought to the next level. You actually start visualizing what it is that you want. This "The Pool Of Enlightened Samadhi" visualization will take you out of the realm of the maya, of the world's thoughts, and bring you into a Divine heaven plane where you will be cleansed of negativity.

Sometimes it's so hard to bring your energy up because lines of attention, or negativity, or things that were just horrible in your life are still stuck to you somehow, and you can't seem to let it go. It's like you still feel like you've got the weight of the world on your shoulders, and muck stuck to you. This visualization will cleanse you. It will lift your vibration, and Light is being transmitted to you as you listen to it. Oh, my Goodness, it is so powerful.

So, whether or not you believe in God, a higher power, the eternal, I know that you believe in love. I know that you believe that you are alive. I know that there's something within you that knows if you could just be helped, or lifted up a little, that your life can be better. At least believe in that.

The Divine lives in you. The Divine knows my intention is that every single person that reads this is uplifted in vibration. That prayer is especially for you as if I were right in front of you doing the prayer. God knows every hair on your head. God, the Divine, has created everything and knows how many blades of grass there are on this entire planet. So, of course, the Divine knows you. You can't breathe, you can't do anything, without the Divine living through you, whether you believe it or not. Truth is truth. You are loved. It is your Divine heritage, your Divine birthright to co-create with God and have a wonderful life.

You are so loved, and everything is possible for you with the Divine.

So, watch the Video Book over and over again, pray and meditate, and soon you will notice more and more peace and prosperity manifesting through the Divine into your experience.

Are You A Mystic?

You may ask, "Why do I care if I am a Mystic or not? I am in my 60's!" Or "I am so young, why would I need to think of such a deep philosophy? I have only just begun my life!" It doesn't matter what your age, culture, or past belief system may be. Finding out who you are in consciousness can shift your entire life to inner fulfillment, joy, and purpose. So, what does it mean to be a Mystic?

Mysticism, to some people, can sound like a pretty loose definition. What is it? Is it complicated? Is it too deep for me? It's impossible to express with words what Mysticism is; however, I'm going to do my best.

A person who is a practicing Mystic is always experimenting with ways to experience union with the Divine. It's pretty simple, but not so easy. It's something that you may have heard in a hundred different ways, but it is still expressing the same Truth. This spiritual Truth, the ultimate reality, can be attained by anybody, although some people call it the final Enlightenment, the ultimate, supreme reality. I won't call it final. It's not. You keep going higher and higher, into faster frequencies of Divine vibration.

There are Mystics from all religions and cultures. There are Christian Mystics, such as Saint Teresa of Avila and Saint John of the Cross, one of Saint Teresa's main disciples. There are Hindu and Buddhist Mystics; in fact, all religions have had Mystics. All religions teach us to be closer to God, in communication with the Divine of our understanding. Mysticism isn't rooted in superstition or dogma. A Mystic is simply longing for communication with their Divine Beloved, and eventually Enlightenment, the Divine Union.

Here are some questions for you to find out if the Mystical path is your path:

Question #1:
Do You Love To Read About And Experience The Unknown?

You ask yourself, "What is the meaning of life?", "What is the secret to all of this?" For a practicing Mystic, the world is expansive and magical, and the unknown is simply something to be uncovered. That's why certain things that you hear will give you a Satori, a knowing. It will ring true to your heart and to your soul, even if it does not make logical sense. You feel the mysteries of life come into your very being as Truth, as reality. This is because you already possess that certain level of consciousness where you've always found that you're quite psychically sensitive. You're sensitive to how others are feeling, and you think there must be more to this life.

Question #2:
Do you Long For The Mystical Experience Divine Union More Than Any Other Experience?

You know that true knowledge means much more than simply a good memory. You want the experience of the Divine above all else. You may have felt soul-sick in your life and want to know what the intangible thing is that has been missing in your heart. When you do discover it is Divine Union that has been missing, you do all you can to have that direct communication with your own Higher Self. Divine Union is everything, and you realize that this is your true purpose, which is to be absorbed into the Divine Heart. You are ready to release your old identity of the ego because you now realize it was all an illusion.

Question #3:
Do you Feel A Desire To Serve Others, And To Turn Suffering Into Happiness?

I find that people that are naturally inclined towards Enlightenment feel a desire to serve others and to turn suffering into happiness. They want to guide others through life's obstacles and release suffering in this world. In their own lives, they have experienced some sadness and suffering because they don't know why they're here, but they know it's something important. You ask "Why am I here? I've got to climb the mountain. I don't know why. I know I've got to be doing something big in my life, and I'm not sure what it is." You do your best not to judge others. You feel compassion and know that some people seem to have been born on the opposite side of the fence and that their suffering can be changed to happiness. You know that happiness and freedom is possible for all of God's creations.

Question #4:
Were You A Sensitive Child?

Even as a child, you may have possessed creative abilities and special talents that are beyond the maturity of your young age. You did not realize it at the time; however, sometimes, you felt strange, otherworldly thoughts. You loved to look up into the sky with no thought in simple wonder at the beauty. As a young child, you said profound things that adults were stunned to hear from a child. You may have daydreamed a lot and saw and felt things others didn't. You sometimes felt lifted out of your body and you would become lost in the beauty of nature. If other children were mean to you, you would feel lost, confused, and sad. You could not understand anger or bullies.

Question #5:
As An Adult, Did You Hide Your Intuitive Abilities And Wisdom From Others?

You have, through experience, realized that it is sometimes safer to hide your intuitive abilities, seldom revealing them to others. This is wise sometimes; however, it is vital that you do not hide these Divine gifts from yourself. When you recognize your gifts and use them, this is not ego. It is acknowledging that the Divine is working through you. Your life becomes a meaningful journey of Enlightening experiences and a rewarding call to serve others. You may have asked yourself, "Why am I doing this small thing? My spirit is bigger than this." Your spirit IS bigger than that thing. That is true humility, knowing that you're bigger than the thing that you're doing, and there is a much larger vision for your existence. It's not saying that the work you're doing is less than you or the people are less than you, but there's something within you that *knows* you were born to be doing more than what you've been doing. Does this ring true?

When you're on this path throughout your life, there will be times where you value experience beyond anything else. Not just a study, but a real experience of the Mystical is paramount to your heart.

One of the things that I want to make really, abundantly clear; you are bigger than that, but we are still all equal. We don't put other people down. Just because someone may not be, as yet, consciously aware as you are, you don't put them down and think they are less than you. We are just talking about how your Spirit is big and you know that you are meant to do big things. It's not putting anyone else down, let's make that clear.

Question #6:
Do You Make Up Your Own Rules For Your Life?

Your freedom means everything to you, so you have never liked being told what to do, how to live, and how to act. You know being part of the norm will never be your life. Your independence means everything, and if you are not independent you feel deep sadness. Can you relate to hating rules and regulations, even if you followed them, because you knew that saying too much would rock the boat and cause disharmony? Lots of people that are potential Mystics don't understand this. They know they want peace at any price, so they will go along with the rules and regulations and do the right thing. But at the same time, it irks them because they want freedom, and they want harmony. They want people to be in harmony, but they're not going to instigate fights. They'll want to keep the peace. They'll put up with people's crap. It really is doing them harm and it will make them sick in the end because they're not supposed to be doing things from that lower evolution of consciousness. It's not coming from ego, and you're not stubborn for wanting freedom. It's just that you know that you're not a person who's supposed to live by rules or definitions. The Ten Commandments are for children. "Thou shalt not steal. Thou shalt not kill."- no kidding! Well, of course not. Most rules are for adults who are like children. Moses made the commandments because he was in charge of these people who had never known freedom, and who were starting to worship some cow they made while he was up in the mountains and had begun to live in degrading ways.

Question #7:
When You Have Heard Spiritual Words For The First Time, Did You Feel In Tune? Shakti, Satori, Enlightenment, Mysticism, Chakras, Eternity.

You are remembering unconsciously your past life experiences and practices. So, when you hear or read spiritual terminologies, you feel a beautiful yearning to experience what it all means. It does not feel foreign to you.

Question #8:
At Times In Your Life, Have You Done Whatever It Takes To Keep The Peace, Even When Others Put You Down?

Have you found yourself agreeing with others even though you know they are incorrect? You are saying yes, no, and okay simply to keep the peace and agree with people who are ignorant and judgmental. Inside, you know that this is not the Truth for you; however, you have no need to be right all the time and you know if somebody puts you down, it is not Truth. However, be aware of doing this because after a while, you may begin to believe the nasty things they say to keep you down. You start believing the lies that people tell you, because these kinds of people are in lower evolution and want your energy. They want what you have, at an unconscious level. They want your energy. They have no personal power of their own, so they want yours. Their way to gain energy is to steal it from you by putting you down and by saying nasty things; sometimes, they may even be violent. They drain little bits of your Light by doing that: parents, siblings, husbands, wives, girlfriends, or whoever, can do this. You'll attract people that will attempt to put you into a victim mode. Get away from these people. The darkness (the maya) will use people to stop the Light. However, remember the only power that

IS REAL IS The Light; all else is fear pretending to be the Truth.

Question #9:
Do You Have A High Level Of Trust In Your Own Morality?

You have a high level of trust in your own morality, and you do not judge others. That is their business, and your life is your business. Your inner self cannot feel guilty about anything because you are free and live a good, happy life. You don't have to let someone else tell you what is moral or not because you are moral, and because you're a free spirit. The challenge with people on the path, when they're not sure yet of who they are, is that they'll ask others for opinions even when they don't need to ask others for opinions. They think it's honoring someone to ask their opinion. And then the person they've asked will normally say the opposite of what you believe is Truth. Trust yourself.

You want to be free and do your own thing, and you think it's polite to ask their opinions. I pray that you've all been released of that by now! This is a reminder. And we don't have to call them assholes or anything. Just don't be with those people. You ask them perhaps to make them feel better about themselves. This is just putting your own spirit down. Don't do that.

Question #10:
Are You Comfortable With Uncertainty?

Not only are you comfortable with uncertainty, but it also uplifts you. You trust in the Divine. You do not let uncertainty put you into stress or fear. You live in the moment. Sure, you set goals and may make plans; however, you know that the logical part of life is always uncertain, and you can be fluid when things change.

You don't always need to have a set plan. You take action, but you absolutely throw yourself into the pool of life. I like what Ernest Holmes said. He would teach that you don't go to the ocean with a little teaspoon and say, "Oh, I'll take a little bit. Oh, thank you, God. You dive into that ocean of life." You don't always know what the next moment is going to bring, but you don't judge, and you take action. You trust in yourself. You trust in your connection to the Eternal to guide you.

Question #11:
Do You Not Allow Others To Dictate And Control Your Life?

You don't need someone else to force you into doing something you do not wish to do. If someone attempts to stop you from doing what you want to do or attempts to talk you out of something, you will be incredibly strong and ignore them no matter who they are. You know your spirit and you trust it above all others' so-called opinions about your life. Eventually, these people who attempt to command your life and your decisions will drift away. They will look for others to control. When Mystics do what other people want them to do to keep the peace, it doesn't end with a good outcome at all. Why? Because they're not following their spirit. You don't have to rely on the physical, the maya, like most people do. Your Intuition and your perception are deeper. That's why we're attracted to this type of study, because we follow our own Light. We are quite strange sometimes to our families. They may love us; however, they never truly understand us.

So, if you can relate to the above, here is some loving advice if you are new to this path. Please don't put up barriers with people. We don't have to do that. If you feel you've got to put up a barrier, people feel it energetically. They feel that you're putting up a barrier and that you don't want to be with them, and that makes them even more curious. They can feel the Light coming from you and they don't like it, especially relatives. So, they will want to punch through that barrier. Mystics are best to conduct themselves as openly and as politely as possible. Always with humor and joy. We don't get involved in any conversation that is too personal. We don't tell people our personal stuff.

You don't say, "Someone ignored me the other day." Others do not wish to hear your small talk, only their own very small talk that is meaningless. They'll be immediately thinking about how someone ignored them and hence they will ignore you.

Please don't act mysteriously. This makes people want to know more about you. You don't have to build up a barrier. You know that you are always protected. You are God-governed. You are 100% God-governed. Say to yourself, "I AM 100% God-Governed." Building up a barrier isn't the same as re-patterning the mind. You build a certain house within your mind and people can't get to you, but building up what you call a barrier is just the opposite. It actually is like a magnet for people. They think, "Oh, my goodness. I've got to get there. I don't know why. I don't really even like that person, but now I am just too damn curious." The only reason you feel like putting up a barrier is because you've been hurt and you're still feeling some lingering suffering. You have just got to release that hurt.

I feel that we all have a responsibility to assist others in finding their way, but we can't really tell someone what's right or wrong. As I've always said, you are grown-ups. You do what you want to do. Everything that we speak about is a suggestion to help implant seeds of Enlightenment.

You understand that everything comes and goes. You are simply a wave in the ocean of the Eternal. You are humble, but you know that there is something huge within you. Even though you're humble, it's God within you. You understand that you are a conduit for God, for the Divine, but not the source. We're a conduit. It's like what Paramahansa Yogananda said. There was this Teacher who came from India, and Yogananda said he was in early Enlightenment, but not fully awake; but something had happened to this man and Yogananda could see it. This man said to Yogananda, "I am God." Yogananda laughed. This man got grumpy and said, "What are you doing laughing at me? I am God." Yogananda said, "Look. I can see that you've got Light in you, but I don't say I'm God. I'm Yogananda."

We are simply conduits of the Light. Everything is a gift, borrowed and bestowed, but ultimately everything is temporary except for the Eternal. Love is our source—love, love, love, love, love, love, love. We know the power of love is everything. We just love, love, love, love, love, love, love.

Love isn't something that originates in everyone. Not everybody has the capacity to love.

They just don't. Most people think they love, but that's just romantic love, or it's only when someone loves them back. They really don't have the capacity to love. It's something that flows through us to other people, and people feel it.

You are Immortal Consciousness. You are beautiful. You have all the power, love, strength, and courage within you. You are connected, completely one with the Divine. The Divine Presence has gone before you to prepare the way. I give thanks that the Divine is bringing into your experience everything to assist your awakening and to assist your finances and health; everything, because you are loved. So, loved. Always remember that.

I say to you, my spirit, this play of life, and the gift to be able to feel without thinking, matters when we are connecting to our Higher Divine Self. When we only have emotions that are clouded and distorted by past hurts or over the top emotions, we can no longer feel our Spirit.

Sometimes we cannot feel and know what our feelings really are. We wish to understand our lives and our true selves, but HOW?

Meditate, Pray, Live, Love, and know that all things are possible.

The Power of Intuition

Intuition is part of consciousness. Developing our Intuition is vitally important if we wish to be free and KNOW that we KNOW. Logic has nothing to do with Intuition nor does so-called common sense.

In this chapter I am delighted to speak to you about the most important topic to assist you to not only be happier, but also very successful. Intuition!

The most successful people that I know and have had the joy and the privilege to work with have strong Intuition. Bob Proctor, Jack Canfield, Richard Branson, to name a few, are guided by that still, small voice we call Intuition.

As we melt away the ice of duality, we can then tap deeply into the power of our Intuition where we are always clearly guided. With this guidance, our life becomes a glorious, happy, and purposeful experience. Whenever we are doing mind and heart practices to bring more clarity and positive emotion, such as Meditation and affirmations, our minds become clearer and more focused. We are happier, and our Intuition becomes stronger. And I'm telling you, my friend, people with strong Intuition are definitely the happiest souls I have ever met because they can trust that they are guided from on high, and that relieves so much stress.

Intuition is not a strong emotion. Some may say, "Oh, I'm feeling so strong about this. It must be my Intuition." No, it's not. Intuition is a very still, small voice. Just a very gentle feeling. "This is the way to go."

And once we understand Intuition and follow it, our life dramatically changes to the positive. We are guided. Our Higher Self will be speaking directly to us. We will know whom to speak to, when to speak to them, where to go, and more importantly where not to go. This is so profoundly important for any soul to become FREE. We will be genuinely, Divinely guided. So, study Intuition and begin with a few simple tools. Meditation practice, and mindfulness, when followed, really assist us to tap into the power of our Intuition.

You know, scientists have been doing this for millennia. They go into a dark room; they write a question down. "How can I create so and so? What is the meaning of this mathematical equation? What do I do next?" Then they go into silence, have a pen and paper ready, and they wait until the answer comes to them. The greatest scientists I have ever read about practice the power of Intuition by going into silence.

I have been teaching this for many, many years and I have been blessed to work with the most incredibly well-known people. I met them through the power of Intuition.

So, if you want to learn more about the power of Intuition and how to become more successful in your life go to https://www.MicheleBlood.com

The Power of Meditation

Practicing Meditation is the most important part in achieving Success, Joy, and Peace of Mind. The reason we say "practicing" is because Eternity meditates us. We call it practicing meditation until we have the real mystical experience of total Divine Oneness.

If we desire to truly move ahead and have wealth and health flowing, we must tap into that which sustains all of life. If we wish to connect with our Higher Self, and not get into thinking it is our own mind that is creating or attracting what we want, then this chapter on Meditation will assist you to delve into your true purpose in life.

This true purpose is freedom, your Enlightenment. This Teaching is for everyone including those who are new to Meditation; however, it will also remind those who *are* practicing Meditation of the awesome power it possesses. When we practice Meditation, we are consciously connected in silence to our Higher Power.

Although there are many ways to achieve silence through Meditation practice, I will share with you some ideas that will meet your needs very nicely indeed.

Create your own space where you will Meditate. Clean this area completely, as this will release old energy. Buy a brand-new mat on which to sit. Light a beautiful candle. You can use the candle flame to focus your attention. A candle *does* bring in good energy, as does traditional incense. A flower or some kind of lush, green plant is also recommended. If you do not live alone, ask your roommate or partner to please respect that this is your special place. Of course, to sit outdoors on the earth is always clearing for the Spirit as nature is Lifeforce Energy. However, always designate a special place in your home to Meditate alone.

Do not Meditate too often in bed. It will add too much energy to your bed, and you may find it difficult to sleep since Meditation gives you more energy. Meditation is not meant to make you sleepy; it is a focused practice. Visualization exercises are okay to do in bed since they can assist you to flow into a positive sleep. However, meditation practice is not the same practice as visualization. With visualization, we still have thoughts. With Meditation, we are releasing thoughts to experience Divine Silence.

Once you have your Meditation space prepared and cleaned, sit down on your mat, lotus style if you can. Sit up straight, with your arms out to your sides, and breathe in through your nose deeply. Please be sure that both nostrils are clear. Blow your nose, breathe in, hold it, and then exhale slowly through your mouth. Your exhale must be twice as long as your inhale. Keep doing this until you feel peaceful. As you are now sitting quietly, place your attention centered somewhere between the eyes and a little above, and take some word that is powerful to you. LOVE, BLISS, GOD, SPIRIT, NIRVANA and BEAUTY are some examples. Ponder the word you choose. Some of my mantras are: *"As a wave is one with the ocean, I am One with God," "As a ray of sun is one with the sun, I am One with God," "I Love God," or "God's Grace is flowing through me. I am now a clear instrument for God's Grace,"* "AUM," "OM," or my favorite, "OM MANI PADME HUM." Use only one power word if that suits you better. You do not have to be religious to do this. This is about focus and connection. And Meditation practice will strengthen your mind. Replace the word "God" with "Love" if this feels more comfortable to you.

As you are sitting and focused on your power word, your thoughts *will* wander off. When this happens, gently refocus your mind back to the same mantra or word. Feel no impatience with yourself or frustration. No matter how many times your mind wanders, bring it back to that one word.

If you do this simple method, eventually you will find that the outside, intruding thoughts will cease, and you will be able to sit quietly in a peaceful state. It may take days, or it may take months to acquire this steadiness of mind. But it will come if you have patience and when you are consistent.

First, do not attempt to remain quiet for more than five minutes or so unless you feel like it. After a couple of weeks, Meditate for ten minutes. You can continue to increase the time until you can sit comfortably for much longer periods. You are doing this to have a conscious realization of your unity with Spirit or to contact God; you are not doing this to see "Light" or to have "experiences." If these experiences do come, just refocus the mind. If we become too fascinated with these "experiences," we could lose sight of the original intention. Keep it simple. KISS – "Keep It Simple and Spiritual" and remember to smile to bring a happy vibration to your meditation time. I call smiling my *Happy Meditation*.

After you have had a few minutes of Meditation and achieved that feeling of peace, joy, and unity with the Universe, give thanks and go about your day. It is recommended to practice these three or four times a day; first thing in the morning, at lunchtime (noon is best), at night (when the sun is setting, it is a powerful time to connect with God's presence), and then at midnight or just before bed.

When you first begin this practice, perhaps just meditate for five minutes three times a day. Just having the intention of connecting with your soul for 2-3 minutes or 4-5 times a day will uplift you tremendously. This will be a great start. Why? Ultimately, meditating 3-4 times a day, even if it is for just a few minutes, will bring you to a place where you are focused and unified with the Divine Presence all day, whether asleep or awake. Consistency is the key. Before you know it, you will be sitting there for hours in Divine Union.

Even if you are agnostic, look at Meditation as physicians do. It has been documented that people who meditate regularly have lower blood pressure, are healthier, and happier human beings. So, Meditate even if the word "God" is not your thing. Put a smile on your face as you sit down to meditate, as this does assist your mind to feel stillness and peace. Do whatever you can to put yourself into a happy mindset before you sit down.

This Teaching is a simple way to learn to practice Meditation. Before we truly experience real silence, we are all only practicing Meditation. But every time we do this, we do raise our consciousness, even if we do not realize it. In time, we will feel better and clearer, and less clogged and stressed. Meditation is not to be taken in an overly serious tone. Focused, yes, but not so serious. Oscar Wilde said, *"Life is too serious to be taken seriously,"* so LIGHTEN UP! Focus your attention and feel happiness and gratitude. This way, it is a simple and easy way to begin to practice. But do not underestimate its power. And if you do not, at first, feel any connection or peace of mind, that is okay. Just having the intention to consciously connect and feel the presence of God will eventually create peace and joy within you, and everything good will begin flowing your way.

WHY?

Because for at least a few minutes a day, you have chosen to get out of the way and let God in. As you delve into longer meditations and find a method that suits you best - and there are many ways to learn meditation - your life and physical wellbeing will radically change for the better. Oh yes it will.

If you are interested in delving more into consciousness and Meditation, please watch a free video on Meditation.
https://www.themysticalexperience.com/PracticeOfMeditationVideo

If you are having a challenge with your Meditation practice, do not give up. Allow these loving and all wise words by the great soul Paramahansa Yogananda to assist you: *"Your trouble with meditation is that you don't persevere long enough to get results. That is why you never know the power of a focused mind. If you let muddy water stand still for a long time, the mud will settle at the bottom and the water will become clear. In Meditation, when the mud of your restless thoughts begins to settle, the power of God begins to reflect in the clear waters of your consciousness. You will become a smile millionaire."*

How To Become Enlightened

We are here to become free. Enlightenment is our true purpose for being. There are so many Divine exercises that can assist us to be in Divine Union.

The first thing is, we must gain energy. We may be meditating a lot, and we could be exercising as well to raise energy; however, we're still not quite there.

The number one reason that people don't become free, or that things aren't going well in their life, is because they're losing energy. We must oscillate at a faster vibration, have more energy, in other words. We're not talking about, "Oh my God. I've got so much energy." We're talking about energy and vibration. Because when we begin to oscillate at a higher vibration, we have Divine power coming through us, to us.

When we have energy, our God self begins to awaken. Just look around at your life to see where you're losing energy. You can look at your finances, at your relationships, at your body, and at your health. You know where you're losing energy, you absolutely know. The good news is you can do something about it. If you're losing energy physically, then begin to exercise to really gain energy. You gain so much energy, so much Light, from exercising. Release the people in your life that are just bad for you. You're probably bad for them too if they're bad for you.

Release relationships from your life that are draining you, or you might be draining them as well; you must. You don't have all the time in the world. This life is short. It goes by so fast. So, you have to begin your new life immediately. Meditate more consistently. If you've never meditated before, begin to practice meditation and then you will gain energy. The most important thing beyond anything else is to become free. Because as I have said, this life is short, and you are here for one reason. So how do you get all that energy and that Light? Can you do this on your own?

That is a very hard question to answer. If you have been Enlightened in past lives you may be able to, however if you a fortunate enough to find an Enlightened Teacher you will be on a faster journey to the top of the mountain. Find someone who can transmit Light to you. You are here right now watching the Video Book or reading this because you are interested in freedom. There's something within your soul that knows Truth. So maybe you're at a higher evolution, and you know that when you have that feeling of wanting Truth, it's because you're searching;

you're soul sick. You're searching for God, for Light.

I remember when I was like that. My heart was out there, glowing, and I thought it was just normal to have this sort of "heart glow", as I used to call it. I went to so many different countries looking for someone who knew God. I didn't really know what Enlightenment was. I'd heard of it, but I knew it was sort of like a Buddhist thing maybe. I knew I was looking for someone who knew God. I was brought up a Catholic, and I actually had a wonderful experience growing up as a Catholic. I was with beautiful Irish nuns and lived in the countryside. It was wonderful.

And I loved to see people happy. When people weren't happy, I couldn't understand it. I would say to myself, "These people have got to be happy. You've got to be happy." As a young adult, I realized that my happiness was to find God. I knew that to find God, I would have to find someone who knew God. Later I realized that that is what Enlightenment is. So, I went to many, many different countries. I lived in Malaysia for a while, and I worked with the great, wonderful soul Bob Proctor, Deepak Chopra, Wayne Dyer, and Louise Hay. I was a speaker and a singer and traveled the world working with all these great speakers. It was wonderful.

However, it wasn't enough. These people were wonderful and some of them were very in love with the Light, with God. However, they didn't know God. I could feel that they didn't. They had a love for God, but I wanted someone who had a union with God, an actual union. So, I was exceptionally blessed to meet an Enlightened Teacher. I had searched the globe for over 12 years, and I finally met my Teacher when I walked into an event she had in San Diego. And thank God the Spirit guided me to come to America because there she was. I have seen gurus and different people all over the world, and I had sat in front of a couple of Indian gurus who were Enlightened. But it wasn't for me. It didn't quite fit. Maybe because it was a different language and culture. Both didn't even speak English. I don't know what it was, but it still wasn't for me. So, I did find a couple of people who had that conscious union with God, called Enlightenment, called a Kundalini Awakening, whatever you choose to call it.

But my Enlightened Teacher was a Western woman; a beautiful, young woman. And when she put her hands up, I saw Light glowing out of her hands. I was looking around to see if anyone else saw that. My eyes were watering up, and I was dazed and blissed out, "What is going on here?" After all those years of searching to find God, I realized that all that Light that she was transmitting was what had been missing from my path. I had to find that person who was in union with God. And in this beautiful form; funny, outrageous sometimes, so loving, so strong, and powerful. But I would always be blown away and think, "How is there so much Light coming through this small woman?" Before I started understanding it, it would just blow my mind. It kept blowing my mind, thank God.

And so, I did everything that she said to do. And I could feel, when I was practicing my meditation, that Light coming through me. I could feel tingling at the top of my head, and I was feeling a heart glow. I didn't realize it at the time, but the reason I had a heart glow was because my heart chakra had already been partially activated from past lives and I was born that way. So, meeting her and having this Light transmitted, I could really meditate deeply.

Being able to tap into someone's consciousness who is in union with God is the fast road. And it wasn't always easy, but it was worth it a million times over. The ego can become very, very, confounded and agitated. "What is going on here? I don't want to die." Eventually, I started having what I call Stargate experiences where I would just take off. Bees would be buzzing in my head, there were huge sounds, and then I'd be flying through this Stargate, just like the TV show.

I'd be off into these different dimensions until eventually one day, one blessed day, the Kundalini completely went out my Sushumna, my crown chakra, and everything exploded into Light. It's all so simple. But it would never have happened without that amazing, amazing Teacher Kundalini.

And I thank God for her being born. Every day I feel the love for my Teacher, and for everything that she has gone through in so many past lives to uplift others, and then for her to go out and Teach to assist others. So, I recommend that you do all the things that I talked about. Exercise your body, eat a healthy diet, read positive books, do affirmations and intentions, and do all the things that will bring you into a high consciousness.

Please do not complain. Love your neighbour as yourself. Your Divine presence is the same Divine presence inside, well not inside the body, it is omnipresent, with everybody. It is the one omnipresent Light, and it is yours. So, I recommend you find yourself an Enlightened Teacher. If you don't come to me, then please do find somebody, because you don't have all the time in the world. It is really challenging to attempt to do it on your own, which I had attempted to do. Trust me, I really did. Just do whatever it takes to become free. Because once you're free and all the fears are gone, you can see the world exploding into Light.

Everything is liquid Light. And you've got this hum in your heart, in your body, all the time. It doesn't matter what you're doing. You're in bliss.

If you'd like to find out more about what I do with my Teaching, you can go to
www.TheMysticalExperience.com

I want you to know that you have all the power, all the Light, and everything inside of you right here, right now to become free. You just require that boost. It's so vital. I Love you so much. God bless you.

What Is Consciousness?

People speak a lot about prosperity consciousness, but what *is* consciousness?

Soul, or Consciousness, is our Higher Self! Joel S. Goldsmith, the great Mystical Teacher, said it perfectly, *"The day will come when, if you know enough about Consciousness you can leave everything else alone, for in the word, 'Consciousness,' and the spiritual understanding of it, is contained all the knowledge that is to be known about God, man, and the universe."*

We who are on the spiritual path, or seekers, are always doing all we can to gain more *Consciousness.* Again, that word? Well before we go any further, if any of what you have read so far on this topic sounds way too out there for you- well, it *is* out there. However, if you truly desire to have success and inner fulfillment, then please do your soul a favor and keep reading. And for those of you who deeply desire to learn more, I recommend you read my book with Bob Proctor, *Become A Magnet To Money Through The Sea Of Unlimited Consciousness*, available as a free gift on The Apple Magnet To Money App. You will devour Part Two in this volume about *The Sea of Unlimited Consciousness* where you will learn how to melt down the ice of illusion and become aware of who you truly are.

When we speak of raising our awareness or gaining Higher Consciousness, what we are saying is that we are doing our best to experience Divine Union. We realize there is no duality. We may understand this intellectually, but we don't know it until we have a true experience of Oneness. We are always striving to have more and more moments of pure bliss and knowingness. Not many people become fully Enlightened in this physical experience; however, we all can. Transmissions do go on, and as we raise our awareness, we slowly begin to melt away the maya and begin to feel our connection with Spirit. Our beautiful soul reveals beautiful Truths once the veil is dissolved and when we are ready to listen.

That is, when we truly begin to understand that *God is closer to me than breathing, closer than hands and feet. Eternity/God is inseparable and indivisible because there is only oneness.*

Whether we believe this or not does not stop it from being true. Those who live in this realization *consciously* find that when any form of lack or so-called opposition comes into their experience, it disappears. This is the true secret of life. The secret of spiritual life. We are not speaking of religion, even though all religions do agree on this one point that *wherever we are God is.* When we meditate, we are doing this to connect with our higher Consciousness, or soul. In silence, this is where true Consciousness is experienced. This is where we are alive in Spirit. Our inner vision begins to open, and we hear, or feel *the still small voice* of our soul. These are the true eyes that see. Some have been able to see with their eyes closed when in a meditative state.

This *still, small voice* is our spiritual guide, and it goes beyond what we *think* intuition is. For true Consciousness has no thought. It is pure knowingness. Stillness. Emptiness. If we wish to begin to get into more conscious awareness of our connection with Spirit, we must meditate, because until we are in the silence, we are only practicing meditation. In today's world, there are over seven billion minds thinking, and we are taking on *their* thoughts. Without going within to the silence, we can find it very challenging to focus our mind, and this is one of the main reasons we get so stressed out and do our best to slip into something more comfortable like a collective coma by distracting our minds with hours upon hours of mesmerizing TV or down the Internet rabbit hole.

Most of the world is in a collective coma, and they don't even know it. Fear and lack do not live in pure Consciousness; it only lives in duality.

One simple way to see whether we are rising in Consciousness is to notice if we are becoming less reactionary. When we react, our ego still holds the power over our lives. When we notice that now we are an observer, a witness, to what is going on, rather than a reactor, we are gaining awareness. When we respond, we are in the moment before we react, and then our actions that follow will be right actions.

Another quote from the great Mystic Joel S. Goldsmith, *"If, on entering a new year, our Consciousness is the same Consciousness with which we came into the previous year, we can be sure of duplicating the previous years' experience. But if our Consciousness has deepened and been enriched, the New Year will be enriched."*

That says it all. Perhaps if Joel had been here at this time on the planet, he would have also mentioned the film "Groundhog Day", for without more awareness or higher Consciousness, we DO live our life and each year the same way over and over again. Just the names change, but the experiences remain the same. We do not have to wait until the New Year begins. We can begin right here and right now. Begin to meditate, stop watching so much TV, and focus on

Light, on conscious union with God. Indeed, it is ALL about Consciousness, and I will say it again... Remember to smile.

And if someone says sarcastically, "*Oh, look at her/him. The Lights are on but nobody's home.*" Say, "*THANK YOU. I've been meditating.*"

The Pole of Prosperity

What is the Pole of Prosperity? It is using the Law of Polarity and the Law of Vibration in our favour to create what we want into our beautiful lives. Once we love our dreams enough, and then take positive action, then the love we have moves our actions into power actions. Love is the highest vibration there is, and when we do not feel love, we can use our mind to change our vibration, so we oscillate at a faster frequency. Then our dreams are no longer wishful thinking.

Now is the time for us to learn another fast and fun method of the mind to visualize, and that is *The Pole of Prosperity.* Hermes Trismegistus said, *"As above so below".* Lack is on the same Pole as Prosperity, as it is just the other end of the same Pole. Lack is simply our consciousness vibrating at a much slower frequency. Whenever we are feeling fear, anger, or depression we are oscillating at a slower rate. Whenever we feel happy, enthusiastic, and have an attitude of gratitude, we are oscillating at a faster vibration. This has been proven in clinical studies, and yet this was written over four thousand years ago. Truth is ageless.

There are many actions we can take to assist us powerfully to manifest our heart's desire. We can propel ourselves into great, fulfilled success and take quantum leaps of increase beyond what we have ever done before. The Pole of Prosperity is truly so simple, and yet very effective. We do not do this to be ahead of the so-called competition, as the vibration for thinking competitively is thinking that there is lack and not enough to go around. When in fact, there is an oversupply and plenty for everyone. The creative plane of life, which lives beyond the Terror Barrier, is where all real success and change occurs. Otherwise, we are only using our willpower, and that is not enough. Our willpower is important, and we need this as our willpower can assist us to change old thoughts of lack *(the opposite end of the pole)* to thoughts of plenty *(the high end of the pole)*. Then, we are unifying with Infinite Universal Intelligence. This way, we will get ahead of our old vibrations of *"Doing it the hard way"* and break that negative spell. People say, *"Well, that's just the way it is, life is hard"*. Rubbish! Life is beautiful.

The Law of Polarity and The Law of Vibration

These Universal Laws show us quite simply that if there is any lack in our life, there is also another end to the vibration of lack, and that is the vibration of Prosperity. It is all a matter of using the same Pole; one end being lack, and the other end being Prosperity. What we must do is vibrate faster to get up to the high end of the Pole, where Prosperity lives.

So, use your imagination and visualize a Pole with a lever at one end. (You can see it on this Chapter of the Video Book.) See yourself moving the lever to the high end of the Pole where there is unlimited Prosperity. Do this whenever you think about lack and feel fear embracing you. You can do this for all areas of your life: Health, Happiness, Trust, Love. Have a Pole with a lever for each area of your life. When you do this, feel your vibration - *your frequenc*y- going faster and then you are using The Law of Polarity in YOUR favour. No more pendulum swing of experiences.

Your thoughts can control your vibrations
by changing your lever on your Pole

Do this as many times a day as you can. You can even physically move your arm up as if you were moving your lever to the highest end. Then visualize putting a lock onto this end, so your levels stay at the Prosperous high end of the Pole.

Doing this will create magical manifestations

There is such a beautiful prosperity and loving cycle that begins when we are in tune with higher vibratory thoughts. We are tuning our consciousness to a higher vibration using the Pole of Prosperity, and it works so quickly. We also begin to see that what we achieve is also uplifting our loved ones and the world at large. When we create a more positive, larger vision, then this vibration and bigger vision become magnified and positively affects all those around us. This also helps us tremendously to stop our little pity parties, which can only lead to self-destructive thinking and behaviors, which are at the opposite end of the Pole where the lever is hardly moved at all.

We deserve to achieve all we can, and we deserve to allow ourselves to be the very best we can be. Let us set forth the intention of making our own lives great and much bigger. Allow yourself to accept an increase, an increase in abundance, in success, and an increase in spiritual awareness. Begin to practice meditation. Begin positive affirmations. Listen to the affirmation songs. It does not take that much to move the lever.

If this still does not make sense to you, let us do this simple exercise. See a volume control fader that is similar to what you will find in a recording studio. You move the fader up, and the volume goes up. So right now, what level is your fader? 1 or 10? This will also let you see where your consciousness is right now, as far as your Prosperity is concerned. Is it right at the bottom, or midway up? Get the picture now?

So, wherever you see the lever, imagine yourself moving it up. It is a simple exercise, but it really does change your vibration about money. Move that Pole up as many times a day as you wish. You can even actually move your arm up as you do this and yell out,

I AM AT THE TOP OF THE PROSPERITY POLE, YIPEEE!

Perhaps your neighbours will simply think you are exercising or that you have won the lottery. So, think big, get clear on your goals, and move your lever to the high end of your Pole and keep it there. Have fun with this exercise. It is simple, fast, fun, and it works.

For those who wish to study further, please enjoy the audiobook, "Become A Magnet to Money Through The Sea Of Unlimited Consciousness", by myself and Bob Proctor, as a free gift, available to you through the Apple Magnet To Money app.

Put more fun in your funds and Be A Magnet to All Good! Thank yourself for reading. Believe in yourself, for you are an unlimited, spiritual POWERHOUSE! And one more thing... remember to smile!

Six Steps To Achieving Your Goals And Big Vision

Let's discuss in this chapter about how goal setting, when used, will powerfully assist you to realize your dreams into reality. All it takes is focus, attention, and six simple steps.

Over the years, I have taught and written about many different topics to assist you to be happier, more successful and to keep you in a high, positive vibration. This includes topics on business, career, Mysticism, Meditation, and so much more. We have also been utilizing the power of visualization.

Visualization is a powerful way for The Eternal Divine Mind to assist in achieving our goals. What we feel and think about before sleep stays with us. This creates a positive difference to the action we take the following day, and we then experience a more prosperous future.

Goals, and having a firm intention to better our lives, are vital to achievement. Now, let's get back to basics. Many people go about their daily routines and lose touch with the simple steps that assisted us in having the success we are presently experiencing. If you are just now hearing about these simple steps, it will blow your mind how simple it is. Always use KISS -

Keep It Simple and Spiritual. These six steps will, when applied, change your own life so dramatically that you will wonder where these ideas were hiding.

Everyone must have a goal in life so that we stay focused and work towards something rather than going backwards. A goal is a part of your big vision. However, it is not your big vision.

For example, if your big vision is to be a multi-millionaire, ask yourself, why do you want to be rich? Is it so that you can be a great philanthropist, travel the world, or bring more Light to the world so that you will have more time to meditate and do your own thing? In other words, do you want to be rich to have the freedom money can bring you? If that is an affirmative YES, then you, my dear, can do it.

There are specific goals you will want to achieve to have that big vision come to fruition. For example, with our business, our goals are clearly defined and written out for www.TheMysticalExperience.com. We work on our goals by breaking them down into projects, sliced down piece by piece. Your main goal is like a lovely, perfectly baked pie, and each slice is a project to finish so that the pie will be completed. This will give you a great deal of clarity. Most people simply become too confused and then become scared because they do not know what to do next, and in what order. Create your pie in mind and then slice it out.

So now let's go through these basic, step-by-step actions for goal setting. It is simple, nevertheless do not allow simplicity to fool you, as these steps are powerful because they work!

#1 Decide what you want!

We're not talking about your big vision; we are talking about what YOU want.

When you become clear about what you want in all areas of your life, then simultaneously, you will also know what you don't want. It's very good to know what you don't want so that you don't get what you don't want, and you get what you do want. So, what do you WANT?

#2 Write it down!

Now that you've thought about what you want, write all of those wants down. You see, your wishes are part of your Big Vision, and they are also your goals. Very few people actually write down their goals. People sometimes do set goals but do not go through the vital step of writing them down in detail as if they had already manifested. Remember to write them down as if they have already happened. This is vitally important. Approximately 8 out of 10 people who do write down their goals end up achieving their goals. That's very good. I feel this is because sometimes, as we grow, our goals tend to expand and change. Our consciousness begins to oscillate at a faster frequency.

Another important point to remember is to *never give up* as some goals take a little longer to achieve. So be persistent and they will eventually manifest in ways that are so mystical it will blow you away.

I have some goals that were achieved very quickly, and others that have taken longer. However, if you know what you want and you never give up, all will come to fruition. Remember your true Higher Self is with you every step along the way. You are Never Alone. And, as the Divine Mother Meera said, *"The Divine Wants You To Have Everything That Will Bring You Happiness"*. Such true words.

Stay focused, positive, meditate, and exercise. Do all you can to gain energy. Never think about what others are saying. Simply focus on what you are doing and, step by step, the miracles WILL occur.

For some, you may only be 5 minutes away. So NEVER GIVE UP.

#3 Timelines!

Now comes the question of whether to put a timeline on your goals. Some people say yes, some say no, so let's clarify this important piece of the manifesting puzzle.

There is a difference between writing down what you want as if it's already happened, and setting a goal. For example, you have a goal, and it may be for different projects that have to be completed by a specific date. This is the time to set a timeline for projects that will assist your goal to be realized. For example, I'll say, "By September 1st, we will have created some new, positive, global live zoom events". Then we will do all the actions necessary every day to have this happen.

Now when we are talking about our main big vision, we always say it has already happened. Visualize it and write it down every day as if it has already happened. Our 30-Day Turbocharged Goal Setting and Daily Action List eBook has this all set up for you with step-by-step simple instructions.

You can also utilize our Magnet To Money APP to set up notifications. Simple and powerful www.MagnetToMoneyApp.com

#4 Sub-Goals!

We have just covered this in step 3; however, let's go a little deeper. Now we have sub-goals for our big vision.

Sometimes projects take longer to complete because at times our projects involve working with other people who may be taking their sweet time to complete their work, so we must be patient and keep all involved positive and enthusiastic.

Please do not have attachment or disappointment when you have holdups when working with others. Be patient, keep your mind on your Big Vision, and ask yourself, "Is this worth it? This little bit of extra time and work?" If the answer is YES, hang in their friend, it will happen with an attitude like that. And of course you can always attract better people to work with you.

#5 Action Lists!

I highly recommend you make your action list after you have meditated or have done something to clear your mind. Have a shower, exercise, do anything to clear your mind, and raise your energy. A clear mind will bring to you all the ideas that Eternity can offer, along with the perfect solutions.

So, clear your mind, and have a notebook handy for each goal. Write into this notebook all the action steps required to make your goal a reality. This is your ideas book. Write down all the ideas that come to you. If you are in network marketing, it would be making a certain number of calls a day, writing emails, or doing a motivational zoom teleconference once a week. Think of all the positive actions you could be taking to achieve your goal, whether it's writing a book, starting a business, or whatever your IT is. Write down lists, think of everything you can possibly do to take positive, fun action.

I've used this analogy before, and those of you who have used the Turbo Charged Goal Setting Book will know this. If you are going to create a new website, well then, your website is your main goal. That is not a daily action, it is a goal. Buying your website name, writing copy, or setting up audio clips would be some of the different actions for your daily list. Creating a successful website is your goal. Build your website and add free products or articles to build traffic.

Now, getting back to your lists. With these lists, whenever you have an idea, add it to your book. If you must write on a little notepad during the day, and then go home at night and put it in your notebook. Do it! It is good to have all your ideas put in one place, so you don't lose them. So many people will write down ideas and then lose the bits of notepaper, so put it all in your Goal Idea Book, type it up, and keep it somewhere safe. Once you are ready to start acting on these lists, I would like you to then prioritize your items on the list. One of the most important things to do next...

#6 Prioritize your daily lists.

Do the harder things first each day that you have been putting off. Have the more challenging actions completed first thing, then the rest of your day will be in the flow. You will become very empowered doing this and have much more energy for the rest of the day.

This is great for personal goals, as well. You can use this method for anything. For example, if you want to go on a holiday, where are you going to go? Are you going to take your family if you've got a family, or are you going to take friends? When are you going to go? How long are you going to go? Which airline? Are you going to fly first class? Are you going to go on a ship? Are you going to go to a retreat?

Write down all the things in order of priority that must be done to take action on that goal. Do it for your personal goals and business goals. See how it works? It is simple, but not many people take action with positive lists.

Now last, but not least by any means, do some action EVERY SINGLE day for your primary goal.

And next, write down your main goals as if they have already happened EVERY SINGLE day. You can use our Turbo Charged Goal Setting eBook to do this.

So, go for it, my friend! Have fun, and live life to the fullest.

Now it's time for your wonderful new life. Write this out now because when you write it down you are using more of your senses. It makes it more powerful.

My New Life

I _____ am now so grateful and happy with my wealthy, prosperous, creative, successful, joy-filled, passionate, healthy, aware magical life! I Love my beautiful life!

I am now open, available and receptive to receive more happiness, prosperity and success into my life. I am gratefully allowing my Higher Power to express through me as increased awareness, increased money, increased supply, increased love, increased enthusiasm, increased gratitude and increased profit and success.

I am now doing what I absolutely love to do as a _____ and I am earning a great increase in profitable money doing what I love to do.

Positive opportunities and wonderful work continue to come to me every day as I take positive action. I rehearse beforehand in my mind the way I want my life to be. All who are involved, including myself, have profited greatly and continue to profit greatly with all of the new opportunities and joy. All of this and even greater good is happening in my life at every moment!

I am now irresistible to my huge success. I focus in the moment, in the now, so that I am always in Empowered States!! I am literally A Magnet To Money, I Am A Magnet To Success, I Am A Magnet To Positive Opportunities, I Am A Magnet To Divine Ideas, I Am A Magnet To Support as all is within me. I always have extra money come to me every week in totally expected and unexpected, Divine right ways. Every day I expect and accept profitable surprises.

I am so thankful to my Higher Power for moving me today to a higher consciousness, in Divine Oneness, so that God's Kingdom is revealed to me. All in my experience are happy, protected, richly rewarding and successful experiences. I am useful to my creator and to this world.

So much love and thanks,

_____

(sign your full name)

Affirmation Power

The Buddha said, "We Are What We Think. All That We Are Arises With Our Thoughts. With Our Thoughts, We Make The World."

Please NEVER underestimate the power of the spoken word. This may sound familiar. "In the beginning was the WORD, and the WORD was with God. The WORD was God. And all things were made by the WORD. Without the WORD was not anything made that was made."

Here the good book clearly teaches us that the physical universe is simply word in form. Jesus Christ, Muhammad, Buddha, Vishnu, and many other great prophets said the same thing, just in different ways. "Do not judge, lest ye be judged." "Love your neighbour as yourself."

The Divine Presence is so generous, giving, loving, and lives within you. You are part of the loving, omnipotent Divine. The Divine in you is the same in your neighbour. Before you can change the world, you have to change yourself. Change your thinking. We are what we think. It is our faith that heals us. It is what we believe. "What the mind of man can conceive and believe, he will achieve." Napoleon Hill stated that quite clearly.

What have you been creating into your life, with your spoken word? You are the co-creator of all. This news is happy. I want you to be happy with this news. You can now create all good into your life. Forget about luck. You create your own so-called luck. Luck is really just Loving and Learning Under Correct Knowledge. Don't look at any person, place, or thing as your supply. Trust and know that the Divine, Eternal Mind, or whatever you choose to call your higher power, is the source of all your supply. So please let go and let God. And remember, don't take life so seriously. SMILE!

As you sing, speak, and write your affirmations, always remember to smile. Show your teeth, gums, and all. Make your dentist proud. No matter how you are feeling, always remember to smile. It takes half as many muscles to smile as it does to frown. Look at yourself in the mirror. Make a funny face. Put on a clown's nose. Smile! So, as you are singing and speaking your affirmations, stand in front of the mirror, dance around, and really let go. Dress up if you like. Shout it out. This is fun and extremely magnetic. Be fearless. Have fun on your way to riches. You are the creator of all your emotions. It all starts with a thought. It is changing your state of mind. Decide now to have happy emotions and happy thoughts.

You must know at once and without any doubt that you are the one who is choosing fear, phobia, superstition, or sadness. Everything you created is through your previous thinking and has caused you emotional breakdowns. If you want to know what thoughts you had yesterday, look at your life today, your relationships, and your financial situation. How will your tomorrows look? Your health? Your relationships? Your finances? It's quite simple. You know the secret now! Look at your thoughts today... Emotions show up in the body as physical manifestations of your thoughts.

YOU MUST CHANGE YOUR THOUGHTS
YOU MUST BEGIN IMMEDIATELY, RIGHT NOW

Start singing a happy tune. Remember, you and you alone must continually feed yourself positive thoughts. Condition yourself to exist at a higher level of excellence today than yesterday. Get your positive momentum going. It is like your body. You can't go to an exercise class for just one day and expect to have a toned body. You have to be consistent. Society may predict, but only you can determine your destiny. Make your own conscious decisions. As Ernest Holmes said,

CHANGE YOUR THINKING
CHANGE YOUR LIFE

Positive changes can be created in mere moments. The level and emotions you feel can speed up your changes. That's why affirmations to music are so powerful. It helps to speed up the level of vibration. Willpower by itself is simply not enough; not if you want to achieve lasting changes. The affirmations in my books and on my musical albums are not only for yourself. Give them to your entire family, and even to your friends. We even have a special album of affirmation songs for young children *I Can Do It Positive Self Esteem Songs For KIDZ.* Let your children sing along. These young minds will be overflowing with good thoughts, and then they will create wonderful tomorrows. Be the role model, and everyone will want to learn your secret. You can tell them it all started with a thought and a happy song.

One thing you can do immediately is download our amazing, world-renowned app (www.MagnetToMoneyApp.com). Heaps of Affirmations, meditations, a sleep program, and the world famous Magnet To Money Song will remind you every day that you Are A Success! All for the low price of a cup of coffee a month. Hundreds of dollars worth of our best-selling products, all on this one magical app. Our app team headed by the amazing Developer Holly Fallah along with Johnny Endara and Treavor Rogers is truly a joy-filled, positive experience.

WHAT IS AN AFFIRMATION?

An affirmation is an affirmation is. Yes, it is something you say repeatedly. It is a statement of word, thought, feeling, or action which confirms a belief system or patterning that we hold in our subconscious mind. Now, these can be negative or positive. It's up to you to decide to choose negative or positive thoughts. For example, "I am miserable because my hair is falling out." Or, "I am now so happy because I no longer need my hair cut." You see, it's all perspective. Your subconscious mind believes everything you tell it. The subconscious mind is subjective. If you tell it enough, it believes and manifests, through the Divine, that thought and positive state of mind into your reality, into your experience.

From now on, choose only positive statements. Repeat them over and over again. Your affirmations must always be stated in the NOW, for the subconscious mind only knows NOW and must be personalized. If you say, "I wish to be rich and healthy," your subconscious will never know *when* you want it, as you are only wishing. Instead say, "I am now abundantly rich and healthy because I am earning more money every day, and my income always exceeds my needs. Extra money comes to me every week through Divine, Magical, Happy Ways. Every day, in every Divine, right way, I am Richer and

Richer. Richer in Money. I am Richer in Love. I am Richer in Health. I am Richer in Stillness and Peace. I am Richer in Profit. I am Richer in Health and Vitality."

You see, as far as your subconscious is concerned, everything is now. So, saying you want to be, or you're going to be, or you wish to be, isn't now. You must always state it in the now, then set your goal and be specific.

Say right NOW,

I am strong and I am beautiful.
I only attract good in my life.
I Am a Magnet to Money.
Money, Money Loves Me.

You become a magnet to what you are affirming. You are what you think about because thoughts become things. The more you understand, the more magnetic you become as your vibration quickens. When you use positive affirmations, you are feeding your subconscious with positive programming or conditioning. The process is simply planting good seeds of thought instead of bad. If you plant a strawberry seed, strawberries will grow. If you plant negative thoughts, only negative conditions will manifest.

Remember, the subconscious only knows NOW. Affirmations, as well as your goals, must be felt and believed. If they can't be felt and believed, use my affirmation songs or make up your own songs. It might sound repetitive, but I truly want you to get it, whatever your "it" is. Become magnetic with positive thoughts. Manifest your good now. Not tomorrow, right now.

Singing along to musical affirmations are very potent and powerful tools, as every word plants itself straight into your subconscious mind. Even if you are simply listening to the music, allow it to go around and around in your mind. It is like, for example, a cat food jingle. Instead of hearing, "I love my kitty food," when you may not even own a cat, start singing to yourself the Magnet To Money affirmation song, available within the Magnet To Money App on the Apple App Store.

I AM A MAGNET TO MONEY
I NOW HAVE MORE THAN I NEED
I AM A MAGNET TO MONEY
MONEY, MONEY, LOVES ME

I know what I prefer to hear in my mind. Writing down your affirmations is also a very powerful manifestation tool as you are using most of your senses.

Now ask yourself. You have to know this. Not many people will ever say to you, "What do you want?" So, ask yourself...

WHAT DO YOU WANT?

When you begin to write, listen, and sing along to your affirmations, make sure you are affirming what you want, and not what you don't want. Here is an example. Instead of saying, "I don't want to be fat anymore," say instead, "I am now at my perfect weight, looking good and feeling great!", which Bob Proctor and I wrote together as an affirmation song. It is its own program called, "Perfect Weight." Get it now!

> I Am Now At My Perfect Weight
> Looking Good and Feeling Great

Create more joy and fun in your life. Life wasn't meant to be serious, and making money wasn't meant to be serious. Life is happening now, and you are here to enjoy every single moment. Your subconscious mind is a very obedient servant. Be clear that what you ask for is what you truly want to manifest. Otherwise, edit it from your mind. My wonderful, late and beautiful friend Bob Proctor taught me a very quick and easy way to get a negative thought from the mind. Simply say, NEXT Or say STOP!

Next, affirmations are the foundation of your building. Think of it that way. The building is your goal, and your intention is to create. The affirmations support the building so that you can, and will, achieve all of your most loved goals. Continuously feed yourself good thoughts and build up that foundation. You deserve the best! Say right now, "I am the best!"

"I, _____, am the best."

Be careful of what you read. Don't allow other people to think for you. What you generally read about and hear in the news is unhealthy consumption. The truth is, there is far more good in this world than bad. If you were to interview people in the roughest and poorest neighbourhood this very day, you would probably find they had a safe and relatively trouble-free day.

Most of what you read and hear in the news is magnified to sell. What do they say? Bad news sells. I'm telling you now that good news sells and will sell you on having a wonderful and enthusiastic happy life. Only allow yourself to hear good news. Be grateful, read positive books, listen to positive people, and listen to positive music. Very soon, you will find you are attracting, just like a magnet, other positive people and positive opportunities. Actually, negative people may feel uncomfortable around you. Please never be concerned about what people think of you. Most people are only thinking about their own life, and not yours. As Terry Cole Whittaker says perfectly, "What other people think of me is none of my business".

You are part of a universe that is abundantly unlimited. Therefore, being part of this universe, you are abundantly unlimited. Look at all the stars in the sky, the leaves on the trees, the grains of sand on the beach, as well as plants and animal life. We are living in absolute abundance. It is as if it were over-abundant. There is waste everywhere, and whoever told you that money doesn't grow on trees? Rubbish! Money does grow on trees. One form of money is what? That's right. Paper. What is paper made from? Yes, trees. Now other forms of money are gold, silver, copper, nickel, diamonds, opals, emeralds, and many more riches from our abundant Mother Earth. It is a recycling of nature into new energy forms and exchange. Look at all that nature has to offer; the Divine does not skimp! We are all surrounded by abundance.

Write down your affirmations a minimum of fifteen times every day, so that they will grow into a beautiful tree of prosperous thoughts. Write them down and whenever you need a lift, open and read. Feel grateful to The Divine and Focus on abundance.

Write a gratitude list every night before going to sleep. The more you are grateful, the more you will attract experiences to be grateful for in this world. It's simple. It is a beautiful cycle of increase and enjoyment.

When you start feeding your mind positive thoughts, you will attract creative ideas, perfect opportunities, and wonderful people. Yes, you become a magnet to all good experiences, including money. Then, the secret is to take action. When opportunities arrive, get up, and take action. Then, and only then, can you be a catalyst to show others how to experience the same. Be an example. Think about what you say. Know that you are creating your tomorrows with your thoughts today. Yes, I am repeating myself for this is the so-called big secret that The Buddha spoke of over two and a half thousand years ago. "You are what you think. Everything you are arises with your thoughts. With your thoughts you make the world."

I love you, and I know you can do this. We are all from one mind. Feel the love I have for you and the love you have for yourself. We are from the same universe and the same God of omnipotent, beautiful Love. I also recommend you exercise regularly, as this will also raise your vibration and make you feel more positive.

Again, I am going to repeat myself. Only be with like-minded, happy, and positive people. Go to seminars and workshops and surround yourself in success. Surround yourself in abundance. If you must be with people whose energy is low or negative to you, change your thoughts about them. Everyone feels down sometimes, so have some compassion because the reason people get down is because they are in fear. It may be unconscious, but they may feel very, very scared. You don't have to hang out with them, however, please don't be so judgmental. We are all part of the omnipresent Divine. You will probably find as you change your thoughts about people, you will think they have changed. In reality, it is YOU who has changed. Find something sincere to say to everyone, even if it is something as simple as, "How are the children?" or, "You're wearing a nice tie today." Everybody wants to be acknowledged. So, begin today by acknowledging yourself. Say right now, "I acknowledge myself and know my thoughts are powerful."

I, _____, acknowledge myself and I know my thoughts are powerful.

I wish you all the happiness and good fortune the Divine has to offer, which is everything good.

Divine Guidance or Emotion from Ego?

Let's go a little deeper in this chapter. When we make a decision, how do we know if it is Divine Guidance or emotion from the ego? Tricky. Is it true Intuition, and what is Intuition? Intuition is listening. When we practice Meditation, we become more in tune with God—with our Higher Self. When we listen in the silence, we can feel our own inner guidance. The Divine Presence within is Omniscient Wisdom. It's the creator of everything and of everyone. So, of course, if we know it is Divine Guidance, it will be 100% correct. We don't have to think to ourselves, "Self, am I making the right decision?"

Those little bubbles of reactionary emotions that guide us incorrectly can be so confusing. When we feel a strong emotion about something, we can feel that it must be Divine Intuition. For example, someone may think they are in love because they feel so emotional, and if the other person does not love them back, they may think, "I have so much love to give. Why do they not love me back? Don't they know what they're missing?" Yes, they know. They are running away as fast as they can!

When we feel emotion and "we want, we want, we want," that is not Intuition. "Oh, I absolutely know that I have to go to Paris, and do blah, blah, blah, blah." When there's emotion involved, that's not your inner guidance. Your inner guidance is so subtle. It is exquisite. You just know that you know.

So, the more you practice Meditation, the more you have Light transmitted to you, and the more that you use your willpower to pull yourself up and make decisions that you know logically are for your highest good, then the clearer you become. "Do I exercise today or not?" What are all the benefits of exercise? There are so many benefits, so of course you exercise today. "Oh, I'll give myself today off." If you give yourself too many days off from the things that are for your highest, Divine good, you end up lapsing. You go back energetically. It's very challenging to lift yourself up again and to use your willpower.

Once you get into a spiritual momentum and you start taking action, every day, on the things that are for your highest, Divine good, then it's okay to have a day off occasionally from something. But even if it's just a little bit of stretching, it is great to do something for your body every single day. Of course, commune with your Divine Presence every day. Let your Divine Presence know, "This is my time to be in the silence. To be with the love of my life, God."

When you feel more and more Divine Oneness you will always be guided to make the right decisions. You will know what to do, when to do it, and when not to do it. You will begin to resonate in a more positive frequency.

Communication is all about resonance. You are resonating, vibrating, and oscillating at a certain frequency that can be heard. Until your Kundalini is awakened, maybe you can't hear it. But at an unconscious level, everyone feels frequencies. You can even feel the frequencies of the low and high Oms. You feel them when you are walking through nature. You will think, "OH this feels so good." Maybe you get a wave of Shakti.

The frequency you are oscillating at is how you attract certain situations in your life. Situations you may love, or situations you may not love. So, as you oscillate and vibrate at a faster frequency, you begin to attract, just like a magnet, people and experiences that are also oscillating at that frequency, or a similar frequency. Maybe a little faster, maybe a little slower, but in the same ballpark.

When you resonate at a faster frequency, you begin to attract into your experience the people and the things that are also at that frequency. Then your life becomes so fulfilled and happy. You find people that you love so much. You say you love the Divine Presence within them, but that is what the frequency is. It's the Divine Presence. It's so joy-filled and it's so humbling that you get to meet people that are wonderful, loving, funny, and so giving. It is heaven on earth.

Then, if you are vibrating at a slightly slower frequency because you are not using your willpower, you are not strengthening your weaknesses, and you are not practicing your meditation, you think you are staying at the same place, but you are not. You are going backward. That's why you see a lot of people that are older that are really grumpy and unhappy because they kept vibrating backward.

You never stay in one place. You are either moving forward, or you are going backward. No one stays stagnant, even if they think they are. You may think you are staying stagnant because you are experiencing the same experiences over and over again that you don't want, each with a different name, with a different hat, or in a different city. That means you are not stagnant; you are going backward.

I want this to wake you up to the fact that you don't have forever. In the timelessness, this life is over in the blink of an eye. Please don't take it all so seriously; just take action to improve your life. Do the things that you don't want to do sometimes, and then you'll find that when you do them you actually begin to enjoy them. You love washing up immediately. You love exercising. You have to use your willpower to take action.

Most people on the planet don't realize that through their vibration, through their frequency, they are creating and attracting into their experience the things that they don't want. Then they blame it on their upbringing or their culture, and they start blaming it on everything. They don't understand that it's because of past lives. We don't need to get so esoteric about this. It's very simple.

K.I.S.S.
Keep It Simple and Spiritual.

If you wish to commune with people and have harmony in your relationships, you can't blame other people and say, "Oh, I've got to get rid of them because they are negative." How would you know that they are negative unless it's within you?

The things that are released from our lives are released from our consciousness and being. There may be times where you truly don't understand why someone is mad or angry because it's not within you. The thing that is in them, isn't in you. But if you get upset, reactionary, and judgmental, or if people are not nice to you and you become upset, it's because it's within you. If you see things that are happening and you are reactionary, it's within you, and it must be released. That is one of your weaknesses to be released.

Allow the Light to release them; to dissolve them. This is what being mindful is. Become aware of your emotions, your judgments, and your reactions. It's becoming aware, "Oh, that's me. It's not the other person. I can't blame them. I'm responsible. I can't judge anything anyone else does. I can't tell anybody else what to do or not to do." Anytime you are being judgmental, it's within you. What is it that annoys you?

If things are happening in the world, we are not to become reactionary. We instead feel compassion and take action to do something and stay calm. BREATHE! Give to the Red Cross or the Salvation Army. Help the people who are doing something to release the suffering on this planet. Visualize positive outcomes for anyone who is suffering. Be grateful for life. Be grateful to loved ones. And always be grateful to The Divine Presence.

Psychic Phenomena versus True Intuition

I spoke about Intuition in many of the chapters of this Video Book and Book, however in this chapter we are going to go into much more detail. There will be some information that I'm repeating because it is vital for you to get this embedded into the treasury of your heart which is your subconscious mind.

Intuition is part of *consciousness;* however, it is not pure consciousness. Developing our Intuition is vitally important if we wish to be free and know that we know. Logic has nothing to do with Intuition, nor does so-called *common sense.*

As we melt away the ice of duality, we can then tap deeply into the Power of our Intuition, where we are always clearly guided. With this guidance, our life becomes a glorious, happy, and purposeful experience. Whenever we are doing mind practices to gain more clarity and positive emotion, such as meditation and affirmations, our minds become clearer, we are happier, and our Intuition becomes very clear. People with strong Intuition are invariably happy souls because they can trust that they are guided from on high.

When we understand, what Intuition is as opposed to an emotion we are feeling, our life will dramatically change. We will be guided. Our higher self will be speaking directly to us. We will know whom to speak to, when to speak to them, where to go and where not to go. This is so profoundly important for any soul to become Free. We will be genuinely, Divinely guided. So please study this and begin with a few simple tools. Meditation practice and advice when followed, are all that's required to help us tap into the Power of our Intuition.

Intuition is so beautiful, simple, and profound. We will experience Spiritual growth, and it will assist all areas of life, including our career and purpose. Intuition is the Infinite Intelligence speaking directly through us, to us!

Intuition means we are IN TUNE with God.

It doesn't matter what we choose to call God. We can call it our Magical Being, Spirit, Love, Higher Self, Eternity, Divine Presence, Our Diamond or Infinite Intelligence. When we are awake to our Intuition, we are awake and in tune with God. Duality is gone for a small amount of time, and we are unified. All the knowledge and creative ideas that have ever existed are totally available to us when we take the time to stop and listen. This is great as well for writers, or anyone in life. It's so important because when we are *in tune,* our creativity flows, and we don't have any blocks. *Yes, no more writer's block!*

While we are speaking of writer's block, here is a quick bit of advice to assist you in your writing and creating. Profound studies and insights into how the brain operates have been made in the last decade. One of them is that it is essential for our creative flow to keep the body well hydrated. Even when the brain is dehydrated by only 10%, our brainpower diminishes by 30%. So, sometimes you might think you have writer's block, and you might *simply need water,* so stay hydrated.

Remember that Intuition is your soul directing you to all the good and all the success in your life. Please understand creative visualization, which is sometimes referred to as guided meditation, is an excellent practice to clear the mind from all the gunky thoughts out there that weigh us down. We literally become clogged. It is like ice surrounding the body, and we must melt away that ice to become clear.

Two of the most powerful ways to achieve this are to have regular physical exercise and daily meditation. Meditation helps clear the mind so that we can allow our Intuition to be clearly 'heard'. In a guided visualization, we learn how to relax the mind and allow someone else to speak to us and to guide us; we start focusing on what we *do want* to manifest into our magical lives. What is also recommended after a guided visualization is simply to be still. Learn how to breathe deeply, relax, and focus the mind. It is best to do this sitting up. This is especially true if you have not done any sort of visualization or guided meditation before. It takes a bit of practice to quiet the mind, and a visualization program is a great place to start.

Remember to inhale through your nose, hold it, and exhale slowly through your mouth. Just keep breathing. When we learn to stop thought, it feels that our higher voice is knock, knock, knocking, and at last, we can open the door. When we don't slow down and become quiet, we can't hear the knocking to open the door where all the answers are waiting to guide us to our next level of consciousness, success, and happiness. When we are silent, this awesome Power can be heard or felt speaking to us and through us. We must learn to be still long enough so we can hear and feel our Intuition. Also remember the importance of breathing, of gently focusing on our breath.

Intuition is not a strong emotion because when we feel emotional, it is usually our old thoughts and habits. Strong emotions are old paradigms. Old paradigms are our old thinking, old tapes in our mind being triggered by a situation in our human experience.

Intuition is that still, small, quiet voice. It's a knowingness. So, when we have a lot of emotion involved, it's usually not going to be our Intuition. Emotions are not feelings; they are the ego. Intuition doesn't seem to have any emotion, and yet it does feel peaceful. It's just a thought that silently comes to us—a quiet knowingness and guidance. When we have that *knowingness,* we have peace of mind and trust. It's simply beautiful. It's Mystical!

A Mystical Experience is Divine Union; it is God speaking through us, and that is Intuition. Our Higher Self is on duty. A psychic experience is all the different thoughts that we are picking up from the collective unconscious. What is the collective unconscious? The collective unconscious holds all the thoughts and emotions from all the people in our area of the world, and we tap into this cacophony of... well, mainly rubbish - *and you thought all that stuff you kept thinking were all your own thoughts.*

How do we know if something we are thinking is really our own thought? Well, this is not important. What is important is that you know whether it feels good or bad. If the thought feels bad NEXT IT!!

People become confused between the two experiences that occur in different dimensions, so let's now discuss Mysticism and psychic experiences. As we just discussed, Intuition is the Infinite directly speaking to us. It is a beautiful and magical power that we can all access and tap into when we pause to listen. A psychic experience is when we tap into other people's thoughts. As a common example, you think of a friend and call them, and they say they were just about to call you. We are all psychic, but that is not Intuition. When we use our Intuition, which is our Mystic connection to Spirit, now that is *real* Power. That's Mysticism. You do not need another person telling you about your future. YOU CREATE YOUR OWN FUTURE! Please know that you are much more powerful when you tune into the Mystical which is your Higher Self, and not the psychic part of you, as the Mystic message is directly from the Infinite, rather than that of other people's thoughts.

You are then totally one-to-one with Infinite Intelligence, *which can never be wrong.* You don't need to go through anyone else. Remember it's all about clarity. It's so important to be clear. What's also important to know is when we are not clear, because some people *don't know* that they *don't know,* and that is disempowering and somewhat sad. So, another reason why it is so important to dispel the fog, the clog from our minds, is so that our consciousness will be clear, which will then allow our Intuition to flow through to our conscious awareness.

When we are taking a shower, the water cleans our aura. Aura isn't just some hippy talk. It's now proven. Neuroscientists are proving that we do have a vibrational oscillation around us, and this vibration *is* in fact our aura or ethereal body. When that is blocked, nothing can flow. Ideas don't flow smoothly, and we aren't able to make clear decisions. So, it's important to use all our tools of the mind to become clear. We don't want to be around people who have muddy minds and think negatively because their advice is not to be trusted as it is fear-based. I know that when we are communicating with other people, if those around us are clear, we are not going to be manipulated by other people's fears or false judgments.

Did you know that everyone is intuitive?

It's not some great gift bestowed only upon special people. Everyone has Intuitive abilities. It's just that sometimes we are clogged. We are living in a fog, and we must dispel that fog to let our Intuitive powers flow through. Some people might say to someone, *"Oh, that person's really psychic."* Well, everyone's psychic. We all have a sixth sense. We can all pick up on the energies that are happening beyond the physical, that is no big deal. But oh, the Power of tuning in to our Intuition is beautiful and can be trusted. Listen to your heart, not your head. Know that we never need to be afraid of what life has to offer if we are looking inward with Spirit because we will *know* that we are always Divinely guided. All we have to do is stop and listen.

Please use your Intuition. Learn to meditate and use creative visualization. Learn to be still. Be on your own more often. Turn off the TV and be still. It's essential to clear the mind. Get rid of the muck. Be out in nature as much as possible. When our minds are clogged, we cannot think clearly, and often we are not even consciously aware of this clogging. Anytime we are feeling fear and not experiencing true joy in our hearts, that is the time we know to stop, breathe, and begin to do something different. Maybe go to see an uplifting movie, take a walk in nature, or meditate. Have beautiful natural plants and flowers around you because they help clean your air and give you pure oxygen and good energy.

So, tune into life from within...

Six Methods To Uplift Your Vibration

#1 Reinvent Yourself through Visualization.

In The Magnet To Money App (available on the Apple App Store), you receive "The Magnetic Creative Visualization Program." This audio program is a fun and an excellent method to begin to utilize your muscle of visualization and imagination. When we begin to use our imagination and visualize who we can become, miraculous things begin to shift. We must be open and receptive to receiving new ideas and all good to manifest, and to remember, that all things are possible with the Divine Mind.

When we can visualize something, it really does raise our consciousness so that we can begin to see new opportunities to see ourselves in an entirely new light. We may see our career expand or experience new solutions that miraculously appear so that we can work from home and make extra sources of income. We must think outside of our habitual comfort zone. Visualize what you do want, NEVER what you do not want. You can put pictures on a vision board. People have been doing that for years, but not everybody does them. I've done them for years, and everything has manifested. Vision boards are very powerful.

You reinvent yourself through visualizing what you want. You allow that creativity to come through you. Think about the question, "What can I do?" As the answers come, visualize yourself doing those things. Put it up on a poster board and visualize yourself being reinvented.

Visualization is very important because we think in patterns and pictures. The mind does not know what a picture is compared to something solid or real.

A photo of one of my cat's faces was printed on a large and oversized pillow. When my other cat saw it, he freaked out, because he thought it was a real, alive, very large cat. He couldn't tell the difference.

#2 The Magic Of Affirmation Power

Buddha said, "We are what we think. All that we are arises with our thoughts. With our thoughts, we make our world."

This is Truth. Your thoughts, when used as positive affirmations, will guide you to new ideas, and higher vibrations will affect everything in your life in magical ways.

Well, what are affirmations?

An affirmation is a positive statement you say to yourself about yourself. It must be stated in the now, and of course, must be positive. The beautiful thing is, in the past, you had to emotionalize an affirmation for it to be planted into the treasury of your subconscious mind. You don't have to emotionalize it when you combine the affirmations with music. When you do not believe an affirmation is true, it is very challenging to emotionalize a positive affirmation. So, with music, it is a whole-brain experience and works very fast. I had this epiphany of doing the affirmations with music back in 1987. This is how my body was healed from a near-fatal car accident.

You can still do affirmations even if there is no music with them, especially when they are done with others as a group. It still uplifts and sends Light to the entire world. The mantra "Om Mani Padme Hum" is also an affirmation. You are affirming that there is Light everywhere, and that God is in the lotus of your heart.

The great James Brown sang, "I feel good, and I knew that I would." That is, I think, the best affirmation song ever written. It's stated in the now. "I feel good because I knew that I would." Anything that can uplift you, affirm it. You do create your reality this way. It is the most powerful and yet simple form to vibrate at a higher frequency.

This is why I wrote so many of my affirmation songs to cover many topics. "I Am Healed", "I Am A Magnet To Money," "I Will Persist Until I Succeed," "Success," "I Am Energy," "I Am Love," "Divine Love." There are so many songs and albums, such as "Songs For Success" and "Songs For Motivation," that you can get on iTunes, including my favorite songs on the newly released album, "Create Miracles - Positive Affirmation Songs To Harmonize Your Life."

Of course, the "Magnet To Money" song is included in the magnificent Magnet To Money App, along with many affirmations that will uplift you.

#3 Meditation Practice

Meditation is so important. Practicing meditation is one of the most beautiful things you can do for yourself and for the world. If you have not practiced meditation before, all you have to do is go to www.TheMysticalExperience.com and download my video, "The Practice Of Meditation."

It's a great video for people who may have dabbled in meditation but didn't really have formal training or a True Enlightened Teacher. You don't have to be religious to practice meditation. It absolutely assists your immune system, it brings your stress levels down, it brings your heart rate down, and it brings your blood pressure down.

Once, I had a medical check-up, and the doctor said to me, "Your blood pressure is so low you are nearly dead, or you practice meditation." Smart Doctor.

You can then go into a deeper meditation practice to find out who you are when the world is in silence. Now more than ever before, is a perfect moment to open yourself up to your true Higher Self. It is beautiful to practice meditation. Of course, there is a lot of music that you can meditate with that can assist in blocking out the rest of the world. However, going into silence is profound.

When you go into the practice of meditation, you can sit in a chair. You don't have to know how to sit lotus style, just breathe.

Meditation also helps you reinvent yourself because when your mind is silent, the Divine can then speak to you, and you will actually hear the still small voice. Your Higher Self can guide you. Your intuition becomes stronger because your intuition is you being in-tune with God, your Divine Presence.

#4 Gratitude

The more things you have on your list to be grateful for, the more things you will manifest that you are thankful to receive. It just works perfectly. I recommend you write out your gratitude list twice a day. However, if you don't want to do it twice a day, please always do it in the evening. Get yourself some paper, an exercise book, or a Mystical Greeting Card (www.MysticalGreetingCards.com).

You then write down six things you are grateful to receive as if you already have them. You can put more than six. You can put one hundred things you are grateful for and to, however, do please write a minimum of six. Always say THANK YOU FOR MY BEAUTIFUL LIFE.

Write down people you are grateful for and things you are grateful for in your life. It is also important to be grateful for things that haven't happened yet, that you do want to have in your experience. When you put a sprinkling of affirmations in with the rest of your gratitude list, the subconscious mind does not know the difference.

The subconscious mind doesn't know the difference between you looking at a picture, or if you are looking at the real thing. Even if you are not feeling it, if you are saying, "I am so grateful that I have perfect health. I am so grateful that I am wealthy in all aspects of my life. I am so grateful that I am calm and peaceful", the subconscious mind will still absorb it.

Maybe you aren't calm and peaceful, but you can affirm it. What you tell your mind does end up being your experience. It is essential to affirm this because then you are focusing on the good.

#5 Exercise and Laughter

Laughter strengthens your immune system. It changes everything. The same thing happens when you exercise. Your endorphins come alive, and you feel better.

Exercise every day. You can do jumping jacks, or you can dance to K.C. and the Sunshine Band. The younger ones are saying, "Who is K.C. and the Sunshine Band?" Also, James Brown.

Watch Monty Python. There are so many Monty Python skits online. Read a funny book, but make sure they are really writing funny things. You can watch "The Ruttles." You can go online to YouTube and watch "Faulty Towers" and "Monty Python" films. If you are not into English humour, you can watch Steve Martin movies from the 80s or "I Love Lucy," or Carol Burnett. Whatever you find really silly and humorous.

Laughter is an instant, immediate method to uplift your entire spirit. The other things we've spoken about don't just uplift you; they change you. You do become reinvented because you are changing, not just your state of mind, but the love in your heart. Everything rises. You feel oneness with everything.

#6 Doing Something To Uplift Someone Else

Another thing you can do that will really uplift you fast is doing something to uplift someone else and doing something to make somebody else happy. Taking positive action every day to do something to inspire and uplift others is so fulfilling. You will even sleep better. We don't share what we do for others; this is not to feed our ego. Giving to others helps uplift you. You get 100 times more than what you gave because you know that it's the right thing to do. When someone has less, and we can do something to assist them, to uplift them, we give.

Give a smile, laughter, money, or toys to orphanages. You can buy them online and just send them, whatever you can do to assist people that aren't as well off. Or to just uplift them with a smiley emoji and funny video clips. Anything really. The thing is to do it EVERY DAY.

When you combine all of the above, and it doesn't take long to do them, you will be uplifted. You will be changed. You will experience greater opportunities, and extra sources of income will come to you magically and more. Why? How? Because you are uplifting your spirit, your oscillation, your vibration, your frequency. Your frequency is vibrating at a higher, faster speed.

So, then your life will be absolutely wonderful and magical, and you will be able to uplift others easily. You will be able to discern what is true and what is fake. You will know what to do and when to do it.

Remember fear is not real. It is something that may or may not ever happen. It is a state of thinking in the future. IT IS NOT REAL. Be in the moment and fear will disappear.

Again, as a reminder, if you have this eBook, print book, or audiobook without already having the Powerful Video Book, you can go to the following link to get the Manifestation Through The Power Of Mysticism Video Book at a discount. Just go to:
www.MagnetToSuccess.com/ManifestationVideoBook

Then add the Video Book to your cart. On the checkout page click the link that says "Have a coupon? Click here to enter your code" and enter the following coupon code on the checkout page.

More Love *(Is the code)*

Link To Download All The Affirmation Songs

Here below is a link to download all of my great and positive, worldwide, successful affirmation songs that are at the end of this Video Book after every chapter.

TheMysticalExperience.com/AffirmationSongs

Our MAIN WEBSITES

The Most Anticipated
Money Manifestation App
Is Now Here!
www.MagnetToMoneyApp.com

For all of Michele's transformational
Books, Audiobooks, Magnet To
Success™ Affirmation albums
and Visualization programs
please go to:
www.MagnetToSuccess.com

www.MicheleBlood.com

THE MYSTICAL EXPERIENCE™
www.TheMysticalExperience.com

**Vibrate at a higher frequency.
Ignite Your True Unlimited Potential and Experience Success in Life Through Transformation of Consciousness with this life changing platform.
Since 2003 transforming thousands of lives.**

How can we transform our lives?

Through transforming our consciousness. Can we do this alone? Yes, however it is a very difficult path to take alone. Here at the Mystical Experience, you are prayed for every single day and sent transmissions of Light Energy (Shakti).

Here in the Mystical Experience™ it is our goal and positive intention to strip away old paradigms of false beliefs and become one with our true Higher Self. And hence our Divine Destiny is at last revealed in all its glory! There is much given through this membership in Divine vibrational energy transmissions, exercises, videos and more.

Do you wish to have harmony, happiness and fulfilling success? You can wake up to who you truly are. ALL things are possible. The natural evolution for all sentient beings, and that means YOU, is ENLIGHTENMENT! If you feel you want evolution in all areas of your life, then watch our FREE videos at...

www.TheMysticalExperience.com

The Most Anticipated Manifestation App Is At Last Here!
The Magnet To Money App
For iPhones & iPods

Read 5-Star Reviews Here:
MagnetToMoneyApp.com

You Can Become A Magnet To Money

- Faster Than Any Other Manifestation Method
- Recharge Your Morning with 8-Minute Wealth & Success Meditations
- Fall Asleep to Words of Prosperity and Love

- Increase Your Wealth & Good Fortune for 2023!
- Have True & Lasting Success Through Higher Consciousness
- Transform Your Mind to Attract Wealth

You Are a Magnet to Money - Let This App Show You How

Scan This QR Code

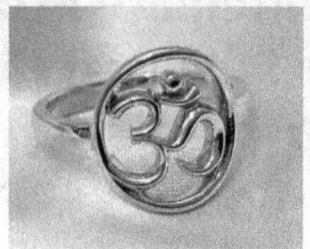

Check Out Our Positive Manifestation Etsy Shop!

ETSY.COM/SHOP/MANIFESTATION4YOU

Spiritual Jewelry, Mystical Greeting Cards,
Affirmation Music, & Other Items
To Remind You To Stay Positive!

MY POSITIVE INTENTIONS

MY POSITIVE INTENTIONS

MY POSITIVE INTENTIONS

MY POSITIVE INTENTIONS

MY POSITIVE INTENTIONS

MY POSITIVE INTENTIONS

MY POSITIVE INTENTIONS

MY POSITIVE INTENTIONS

www.ingramcontent.com/pod-product-compliance
Lightning Source LLC
Chambersburg PA
CBHW050254120526
44590CB00016B/2348